SPELL CHECK

Lessons Learned from Screwing Up Words

Spell Check: Lessons Learned from Screwing Up Words
Edited by Caitlin M.S. Buxbaum and Colette Freedman

Library of Congress Control Number: 2025927824

Title and chapter headings set in American Typewriter ITC Pro
Publishing company name set in Elephant
All other text set in Neue Haas Grotesk Display Pro

First Edition, Corrected

ISBN-13: 978-1-959525-98-1

SPELL CHECK

Lessons Learned from Screwing Up Words

edited by

Caitlin M.S. Buxbaum
Colette Freedman

Red Sweater Press

Wasilla, Alaska

2026

Table of Contents

Introduction

Hello! I'm Caitlin Buxbaum (née Skvorc).

There are three things you need to know about me before you read this book:

- I have always been a writer.

- I have always been "good at school."

- I was born and raised in the United States, and English is my first language.

Given these facts, it should come as no surprise that I participated in spelling bees from the time I started school until I reached ninth grade, when I no longer attended a school that hosted such events (the upper age limit for national participation is under 16 or below ninth grade).

If you've never heard of a spelling bee—which I recently learned is a largely American phenomenon, beginning in 1908—it's a competition in which students must spell words correctly, without writing them down. The announcer can provide the definition(s) and part(s) of speech of the given word, and even use it in a sentence for the speller, when requested. The challenge is completed in rounds, and no words are repeated (usually), so if everyone spells their individual word wrong in a single round, they all get to stay and try new words in the next round. But if just one person in the round spells their word correctly, they are the winner.

As a student in small-town Alaska, I was fortunate to win my school spelling bee twice: once as a fourth grader, and next as a seventh grader. Although I haven't laid my hands on the newspaper clippings in many years, and I seem to have lost any elementary school diaries I may have kept, I still remember the first word I lost out on at the state bee: pirouette.

Unless you studied ballet as a child, you may be nodding your head reading that word, thinking something like, 'ah, yeah, that's a tough one for a nine-year-old.' But what you couldn't know without having been there is that the announcer was a middle-aged Southern woman who very clearly pronounced the word "pare-oh-wet." And one of the things about spelling bees is that you are supposed to say the word before and after you spell it, so I said it exactly how she did, and spelled it p-a...

Caitlin Skvork wins the spelling bee and gets to compete in the Anchorage Daily News Bee.

Who knows what came next. Of course I got it wrong. And while there is even an appeals process, which I utilized after that round, I wasn't afforded a second chance to continue in the 2002 state spelling bee.

Would I have spelled the word correctly, if it had been pronounced correctly, without an accent I had yet to encounter in my relatively sheltered young life? We'll never know. The injustice of it all is what has stuck with me the most over the years, as trivial as the event may seem.

Funnily enough, I don't remember any of the words I had as a seventh grader in the school or state bee, but I did write them down in my journal (amidst a hilarious and slightly alarming amount of boy-crazy ramblings, and at least one misspelled word). At Colony Middle in January 2005, my winning word was "quorum," and some of the words leading up to it were muskrat, femur, bagel, probation, adolescence (which I misspelled, along with everyone else in that round, apparently), and impatiently. At the state bee in Anchorage a few weeks later, I "tied for 6th" and lost out on "postcibal," which is a word I had never heard, and haven't since, and which Google Docs tells me is misspelled (if you're curious, it means "occurring after eating").

Fast forward a generation, and I now have a Master of Fine Arts in Creative Writing from Antioch University Los Angeles. I still pay special attention to words and their spellings, having started as a poet and blossomed into a screenwriter under the mentorship of Colette Freedman. During my second-to-last residency, she asked our workshop group to write answers to questions that would serve as the draft or outline of our eventual artist statements. One of these questions was "What are 2-3 formative experiences from your past?" and for some reason, I chose to reference the time I cheated on a spelling test in second grade and got the answer wrong. The word was "forty," which I erased and misspelled "fourty" after eyeing my classmate's paper. To me, the moment was a lesson in integrity that I've carried with me my entire life. But to Colette, it was more. She had just heard me fretting about being in my thirties and not seeing a clear trajectory for my life, hearing the clock ticking against my body and she insisted, "Forty is when you've stopped fucking around and your dreams really start to manifest. It's not too late, and in fact, it's just the beginning for many filmmakers and creatives out there."

As it turns out, many of our friends still remember their spelling bees and the words that kicked them out of the competition, and many of those words are remembered for a reason other than being an early failure. Looking at my most memorable losing word in this context, I can see how I've strained myself in life, constantly *pirouetting*—spinning precariously from one thing to the next, doing too much too fast without enjoying the moment, the successes, the accomplishments.

So whether you're like me and did a spelling bee every year

you could, or you struggle to spell most words correctly (in your native tongue or otherwise), consider: What word sticks with you, or trips you up the most? What is that word doing in your life? Why do you remember it?

These are the questions Colette and I have asked the following writers to answer.

ADDRESS

Colette Freedman

4th Grade. Beth Tfiloh Day School. Maryland.

I got out in the second round of the spelling bee on the word "address." I forgot/didn't know/had no clue that there was a second D. I was out and Ben Braverman or Randie McFeely or Allyson Greenbaum won.

The irony is that I hadn't lived in Baltimore for that long. My address was new to me. I was heartbroken when my parents brought me into their bedroom one day, showed me a globe and pointed to Maryland. "Do you know where this is?"

I immediately burst into tears. I loved living in Wisconsin. I had friends. A cool room. An awesome candy store around the corner. It was my home. It was my address.

"I am never leaving," I bawled. "This is my home forever."

"We're moving closer to Disney World and we can go there," my parents continued.

The faucet of tears immediately shut off... I was in. So much for standing my ground.

Since the move to Baltimore, I've had several addresses and I have truly loved my various apartments, dorm rooms, lake houses, guest houses, and duplexes. They're stuffed with my things: the furniture and art and books and tchotchkes that fill me with warmth and memories. But with the recent fires in Los Angeles and seeing so many friends lose their homes, it's made me think a lot more about my address. Because even if I lost everything, I would still have the memories and, more importantly, the friends and family and community and village representing them.

So, for me, an address is simply where you live, but it's the people in your life that make an address a home.

So fuck the extra D. I spell address H-O-M-E.

ALMOND

Emily Hagopian

7th Grade. River Dell Middle School. New Jersey.

I never thought of myself as any great speller. I had proven that already during my fourth-grade spelling bee when I got out in the first round on "burglar." Something must have changed after that, because I went on to win the class spelling bee in Ms. Pomeroy's seventh-grade English class, as well as the school-wide spelling bee. From that point, I moved onward and upward to the local regional qualifier, in order to compete in the North Jersey Regional Spelling Bee, and then, the holy grail: the Scripps National Spelling Bee.

The regional event took place at the Knights of Columbus building in the next town over. My family came along with me, as well as my teacher, Ms. Pomeroy, who was there with her fiancée. *Why was she here on a Friday night?* Even my Girl Scout troop leader came to support me. *Didn't everyone have better things to do with their time? Didn't they know it was a fluke that I managed to get this far?*

At this point, things were getting too official for my taste. The stakes were rising, along with my perfectionist anxiety. How could I not have foreseen that doing something well would ultimately mean I would be expected to outperform myself every time I did it henceforth?

My family looked up at me eagerly as I stepped onto the small stage. The woman said my last name wrong as she called me up, of course, but I've learned not to correct people by now.

The word was "almond."

My mother always told me my eyes were like my grandfather's, who died a year before I was born. Almond-shaped. Anytime I was handed an old photograph of him, I would search into his friendly face and try to notice any traces of myself, greedy to find some connection. He came to the U.S. from Kuwait, changing his family name along the way to "Hagopian" to better embody his Armenian roots, as well as further the story of connectedness with our past. The name he'd been born with was a remnant of a violent history, when his own grandfather was given the name as an orphan of the Armenian genocide.

Even though all names are made up, they're still deserving of their correct pronunciation. Growing up, I understood the way my name opened up a conversation that could be broached with people I might not normally have spoken to. I felt like it was a burden having to constantly explain myself and my history—like I was translating a piece of myself for those around me into something more palatable.

But what if this was, in fact, a good thing? Having multiple pronunciations of my name meant creating a new version of myself to be explored each time—a new addition to my ever-changing identity, and new conversations to be had along with it.

My word was...

"Ahmun," the announcer says, with a thick Bostonian accent.

"Aman?"

"Ahmun."

"Amen?"

Well...*shit*.

I got out in the first round.

At the end, my teacher beamed at me. She was proud I'd made it that far and tried my "best," of course. This was just a stepping stone in a long line of learning how to fail well. It's a lesson I still struggle to fully embody in my life, but I know it's always worth the challenge.

I don't remember if I asked for the definition or for the word to be used in a sentence; if I did, then this is even more embarrassing. All I know is from that point forward, I understood: There's always more than one way to pronounce a word, regardless of its spelling.

BAMBOOZLED

Ozzie Rodriguez

6th grade. Driftwood Middle School. Florida.

I hate contests. I despise being put up against other people just to have someone else be declared the champion and hold a trophy over their head as I receive a second-place, third-place, or the ever-embarrassing green participant ribbon. But what's funny is that it's not so much that I loathe being challenged; it's that I'm *so* competitive that I hate losing even more. Monopoly, arm wrestling, bar room trivia, fantasy British Bake-Off pools— my immediate instinct is to prove myself and to win. Sadly, winning is not always an option.

Well, it's likely never the option, in my case, and here's why...

Spelling has always come easy to me, in part because I grew up speaking Spanish as well as English. With so many "loan words" and letter sounds in common, being fluent in both of these languages has often helped me sound out words in a way that leads me to spell most words correctly. It's not always effective (think words like "colonel" and "hors d'oeuvres"), but in junior high, it was working well for me. So much so that the English department at Driftwood Middle held their 6th grade spelling bee in the classroom of my homeroom teacher, Mrs. Floyd. I'd never been in one of these before. I didn't want to stand in front of a class and spell out words. I mean, that was for nerds, right? I didn't want to get laughed at. Plus, I was a shy kid, but that was only until I was told by Cuban hippies once that being shy was equivalent to being greedy with my own personality. So I just called myself tortured, but that's another story for another time.

Bottom line, I didn't want to be in this spelling bee. I didn't want to stir up those competitive juices, not here at least. But Mrs. Floyd forced her entire class to participate. Her strong Jamaican accent made it difficult for us to say no to her, mostly because you could never tell if she was amenable or angry. My best friends Robbie and Brian were thrilled though. They loved this shit. They were optimistic they could win, but I knew better. We were up against Thu Dang (sounded like "too dang"), the smartest girl in our grade. We even joked about her name and said she was "Thu Dang smart." There was no competing with Thu around, but it was 1989, the '90s were right around the corner, so, like, whatever. *Let's play.*

My first word was easy. Baby stuff. Only a few students were eliminated; mostly the prepubescent jocks and the Billy Idol wannabes. Second round, I spelled that word correctly as well. More people fell off the roster this time. Bryan, Robbie, and I were still hanging in there, but so was Thu. Third round had even fewer students, some getting physically nervous, since they represented other homerooms, but I still got my word right. Next round, Robbie and Bryan were both knocked out. Thu and I were there with maybe five other kids. The pressure was on. The sweat formed around my wispy upper-lip hair. This is *exactly* what I hadn't wanted to happen. And then, my name was called. I stood up, walked to the middle, and was asked to spell the word...

Bamboozled.

I froze. What the hell was "bamboozled?" Sounded like some sort of muzzle made for a hungry panda. I sounded it out in my head and ran through every orthographic rule in the English language I could think of. Why on Earth was I still playing this stupid game, if I knew I was just going to embarrass myself by losing?!

Bamboozled. B-A-M-B-O-O-Z-L-E-D. *Bamboozled.*

The word I heard next would haunt me for years to come:

"Incorrect."

Of course, Thu would be offered the same word right after me and spelled it... exactly the same way, *except* for the D at the end.

Wait a minute! Mrs. Floyd sounded out the word in past tense! I lost because I heard Mrs. Floyd use the word in past tense! Her accent betrayed me! Outrage!

I've never forgotten that word. Over three decades later, it still makes me question every word I ever write, type, speak, or even think up. I often wondered what happened to everyone in that spelling bee. I heard rumors of Robbie becoming some hunky plumber in Florida. I only know this because Brian found me on Facebook years back, and ranted about him (oh yeah, he likes guys now). I often think about Thu Dang, and whether she's out there making artificial hearts for babies or colliding sub-atomic particles in a space shuttle somewhere (she won, by the way—as if there were any doubt). And I hope Mrs. Floyd is still teaching English somewhere the students can hear the difference between past and present tense. As for me, maybe losing the spelling bee made me the screenwriter I am today. And maybe I should be proud of the fact that I tried something, failed, and still managed to dust myself off and do something with my life, right? Maybe that's the whole takeaway here.

Yeah. I could end there on a high note, if it weren't for my recent internet revelation that *bamboozle* is a word from a third -grade spelling bee list. THANKS Google!

CALENDAR

Tracy Mishkin

3rd grade. Grandview Elementary School. Indiana.

I don't think of the third-grade class spelling bee at Grandview Elementary every time I write the word "calendar," but it happens often enough. Often enough to keep me humble, to remind me of when I wasn't. (My father kept a diary when I was a child. He frequently wrote about how smart I was, and he told me that too.)

As we lined up for the class bee, I assumed I would win. Then I would win the school spelling bee too. My favorite teacher, Mrs. Blumhardt, announced the spelling words. My first was "calendar."

I spelled it D-E-R at the end, and Mrs. Blumhardt gently told me to take my seat. I was flabbergasted. I'm pretty sure I argued with her. (Full disclosure: spellcheck caught my mistake in "flabbergasted.")

About 50 years after I had the spelling of "calendar" burned into my memory, the public library here in Indianapolis hosted a spelling bee. I signed up, thinking perhaps I could erase the memory of my defeat and my behavior. Maybe I could even win.

The contestants were a diverse group of people, including a man in his 20s who had gone to the national spelling bee as a child. While I am a capable speller as an adult, I am not as good as he was. I decided that my goal was to support the other contestants. I applauded each person and argued when I thought someone deserved another chance.

After several rounds, the bee came down to Mr. National Spelling Bee and me. It was pretty fun, and the audience was enthusiastic. Eventually I got some French word related to cheese and picnics, and that was it. Second place felt like a win, so...

I circled the date on my calendar.

DIGESTIBLE

Ty Halton

3rd grade. Bessie Owens Elementary School. California.

It came down to the final two of us. Noah Kroeker (that annoying little shit), and Third-Grade Me.

Digestible. Language of origin: French. Definition: easy to digest; easy to understand. *Digestible*.

None of that helped Third-Grade Me. Third-Grade Me stood frozen in the cafeteria at Bessie Owens Elementary School, as terrified as a firefly in the palm of a bear.

D-I-G-E-S-T-A-B-L-E. And then the bell. I sat back in the cold metal chair and folded in on myself like a crumpled piece of paper, softening the edges to blend into the background, easier to take in without leaving a mark.

Noah's turn. D-I-G-E-S-T-I-B-L-E. Silence, and then...

That is correct! followed by the eruption of cheers and celebrations from Kroeker's friends and family.

My mother always told me that I was a riddle too tangled to unravel, a flavor too sharp to savor. My father said that I left those around me struggling to swallow what I had to offer. I was a bitter herb to my siblings' sweet fruit, a puzzle with no solution. While they were warm, familiar tastes—effortless, comforting, easy to absorb—I was a tangle of sharp edges, an acquired taste, something that required patience and understanding to uncover. Simply put, I was not digestible.

As I grew from a boy into a man, I fought to smooth those edges, to soften my flavor, desperately trying to make myself more digestible—an easy, comforting presence that didn't leave a lingering aftertaste. In doing so, though, I chipped away at everything that made me, me. The fire in my voice, which used to ignite passion and conviction, became a whisper of fear. The boldness that led me to challenge and question was dulled into silence. That spark in my soul, the wild imagination that once danced without limits, was tethered and quieted, as though it had to stay within the lines.

Each piece that I silenced for the sake of being more digestible in the hope that someone would tolerate me enough to love me one day left a little more of me behind, until I no longer recognized myself. I was pouring from an empty cup, fighting for the love of a person who consistently asked me to make myself easier to swallow. I couldn't tell where I ended and where the expectations of others began. I condensed myself so that I could fit in any box, and they still left. Never again.

Twenty-Nine-Year-Old Me looks in the mirror and sees Third-Grade Me gazing back. I offer the boy the love he sought in third grade, and fourth grade, and eighth grade; the compassion he desperately clawed for as an undergraduate. And I apologize to him. And I tell him:

I am no longer asking for permission to take up space.

I will no longer shrink for anyone's comfort, or quiet the

parts of me that stir the air and unsettle the stillness.

If I am a storm, I will rage. If I am a fire, I will blaze. If I am a river, I will flood.

I don't need to be digestible for anyone—let them consume me in my entirety with the care and understanding that I deserve.

Or let them choke.

EGRESS

Teresa Kale

7th grade. Venado Middle School. California.

It was seventh grade. Late in the year, so the teachers were itching for summer almost as much as the 13-year-olds who'd been marinating in the thick hormonal broth of Venado Middle School for the last six months. Everyone was eager to get out of there. Everyone except for me.

I had a spelling bee to win.

I was your stereotypical "try-hard," before that was a popular term. A hand-raising, front-row-sitting teacher's pet. And there wasn't a competition around that I wasn't gunning to win. Unfortunately, the spelling bee was about to hit me in my secret sensitive spot.

I'd been killing it up on that stage until this moment. My longtime academic nemesis, Adam Mirkovich, had already taken a seat, and it was me versus Adrienne D'Luna and Irene Choi, both shy but secret killers. I had all the confidence of a suburban white girl who had yet to face any actual challenges in her life.

You see, I'd always been a big reader. My vocabulary was epic (if I did say so myself, which I did. Often.) But when you read a lot, you're also saddled with a unique Achilles heel. You know how words look but not necessarily how they sound. And this was long before the internet and the cell phone became the mispronouncer's best friend. So I would blithely cruise through life, confidently pronouncing words incorrectly. "Calliope" was "Callie-ope." "Inconsolable" had an extra emphasis on the "con." It was mostly fine, as I was mostly oblivious. But if I made these linguistic mishaps in front of Bits, my older sister and idol, get ready for the peals of laughter and the never-living-it-down.

My worst-ever incident was when I'd seen an intriguing word haphazardly scrawled in the bathroom at Venado: "Fuch." *Interesting*, I thought, ever the word connoisseur. *Never knew that's how that particular curse word was spelled.* It was only a week later that I made my biggest faux pas yet. While perusing adorable purses in Claire's at the mall, I confidently pointed out a particularly lovely magenta one to my sister and, with the utmost confidence, said: "Isn't this a nice fuck-sia color?" Only I said it with the hardest "k" sound ever spoken by a preteen girl. As Bits descended into hysterical laughter right there in the mall, I eventually learned, through her gasps for air, that it was in fact pronounced "FYOO-sha," and that those little middle school fuch-ers couldn't spell for shit.

But all that was in the past. I was about to prove all the haters wrong by spelling my next word...

"Egress."

Egret? Does she mean the bird? No, it definitely had an 's' at the end. What the fuch is an egress? I'd finally come face to face with a word I hadn't read, whose pronunciation might have helped me had I not been saddled with a brain for reading first and mispronouncing later.

"E-G-G-R-E-S-S?" I tremored. "*EHHH!*" my favorite English teacher intoned, imitating the buzzer the school hadn't bothered to procure. "Incorrect. Egress only has one G, Teresa," Mrs. Dann explained. And then, to drive the knife deeper, she added, "E-G-G-R-E-S-S would be pronounced 'egg'-ress." My mispronouncing brain had struck again!

And with that, my confidence burst like the world's most melodramatic tween balloon. As I egressed off the stage (*egress: to go out of or leave a place, you dumb dumb*), I sped to the bathroom to cover my shame. I slammed the stall door shut to have a good sniffle.

Better times would come. I'd go on to write essays and TV shows and movies, all forged from that weird little mind that was still in its nascent stages back in the grimy halls of middle school. I'd mispronounce words on the biggest stages, in front of Emmy-winning bosses and television writers' rooms that were far more ruthless than my big sister. I'd egress from place to place, leaving behind sloppily pronounced, multisyllabic words in my wake where simpler ones would do, merely for the unadulterated pleasure it gave me.

But back then, in seventh grade, I was just a defeated little competitor who had lost in front of everyone, sitting on a toilet in an institutional bathroom that defied all the janitorial staff's cleaning attempts. I looked up at the stall door. And what should I find facing me, in my moment of despair? The very graffiti that had caused my most egregious pronunciation crime to date. In a moment of defiance, I took out my best pen and added a short, black line to that "Fuch," turning it into a gloriously correct "Fuck."

Feeling better, I returned to watch the rest of the spelling bee, never again to compete, but happy to know that I had aided, in some small way, all the future mispronouncers of Venado Middle School.

ENVIRONMENT

Jodie Snyder

8th grade. Townsend Junior High. California.

"No. I'm sorry, it's e-n-v-i-r-o-n-m-e-n-t."

I stood my ground and squeaked out, "You're sure?"

Mrs. Ray looked over the tops of her thick glasses, her stare intent on shooing me offstage.

She sighed and again spelled out my word/nemesis, emphasizing the "n" I had chosen not to use.

I remained still. If the Townsend Junior High student orchestra had been there, they would have been trying to play me off the stage. But they were off doing some kind of U.S. Bicentennial thing. It was up to the formidable Mrs. Ray to keep the show moving. She continued to glare at me and jerked her neck toward the exit, a slight move that had enough umph in it to make her jowls wobble; she wanted me to scram.

I gave her another hard look and walked off, careful not to trip in my polyester bell bottoms or ruffle my feathered hair, floating à la Farah Fawcett.

I walked off to begin my Year of Questioning Everything.

It just so happened this was also the year I turned 14 and experienced my first gusher of adolescent hormones. The aftermath of the school spelling bee and ongoing surge of emotions and pimples added up to what my mother still refers to as *annus horribilis*—a collision of skepticism and sassiness the likes of which the world had never experienced before.

Before going home, I insisted we stop by the school library. I knew my old friend—and perhaps my best friend—would not let me down. The library would have a book that would prove I was right. Circled by my impatient family yet surrounded by the comforting smell of old books, I leafed through the Merriam-Webster New International Dictionary—so heavy it needed its own lectern. And there it was: environment.

I sounded it out; there was no "n" in that word. The dictionary was wrong. Mrs. Ray, my mother, Merriam, as well as Webster, and all other authority figures had it wrong. There was no "n."

As I rode home, unbuckled, in the back of my mother's land yacht, the Ford LTD, I began wondering what else people had gotten wrong. That night, for the first time ever, I asked my mother why I had to go to bed at 10.

She gave in on that one. (It took me decades to realize she had been right, and I do much better with eight hours of sleep).

Groggy from staying up until midnight, the next day I began my quest to find out what else the world had screwed up. All day, I asked "How do you know that?" "What makes you say that?" "How come?" "Are you sure?"

And then I stopped simply agreeing to things. "Why do the dishes have to be washed after dinner?" "Couldn't they wait until morning?" "How do you *know* we would get bugs?" "Have you ever seen bugs in the house?"

I was like a toddler engaging in the Socratic method.

I took my skepticism show on the road and was a general pain in the ass to all my teachers. I still did my homework, but every non-A I received required exhaustive explanation from them. I questioned the validity of homework assignments and frequency of seeing films in class. I wondered out loud how we were going to cover all of America's history in Mrs. Ray's class if we spent 10 weeks on the American Revolution alone.

I wish I could say that my questioning did any good: girls still had to wear hideous rompers in PE while the boys got away with shorts and T-shirts. At least we young ladies were allowed to pull out the elastic from around the rompers' waists, but I'm still not sure how wearing baggy sleeveless rompers helped the cause of Title 9.

Entering high school took the edge off my skepticism. It was hard to be questioning—or even speak out—when surrounded by tall and godlike high school seniors. All my thoughts coalesced on getting to the library and making it home without turning into god roadkill.

Sophomore year, however, I was back at it—asking my parents why they supported Ronald Reagan, why we had to kill the frogs in biology, why we couldn't read more female authors in class. And then, something more magical than people wising up and spelling environment correctly happened: I joined the staff of the high school newspaper, and I was home.

The same scenario repeated itself in college. As a freshman, I was too befuddled to ask any questions (I found the bathrooms all by myself, thank you very much), but in my second year, I became a reporter for the school's daily paper. With every front-page story I bagged, I questioned the need to go to journalism classes and the value of academics in general.

Despite my skepticism about the value of a college education, I managed to graduate. With my front-page clips, I landed a dream job as a journalist for the state's largest newspaper, covering, you guessed it, the *enviroment*.

Or as my editors still insist on spelling it, environment.

EUDAEMONIC

Kady Ambrose

Adulthood. Paris, France.

I've never been in a spelling bee, but I've seen a clip of one on YouTube. A 10-year-old kid in pigtails and glasses correctly spelled the word eudaemonic.

Thanks to her, I now know it's an adjective derived from Greek that means "producing happiness." Merriam-Webster goes further, indicating that it's "based on the idea of happiness as the proper end of conduct."

Are spelling bees eudaemonic for their fourth-grade participants? Is their happiness even the goal? Are there other, more "proper" ends of conduct?

My father once told me he didn't aspire to be happy, which made me incredibly sad. He maintained that happiness is like a sugar high. Contentment and fulfillment were his aim. They're more within our control, and more sustainable. Of course he was right. Experience has taught me that. But I still love me my happiness when it drops by for a visit.

I'm confident that once her spelling bee days are behind her, that kid will never need to correctly spell eudaemonic again. Or anything else, for that matter. That's why God invented spell-checkers. But I'm guessing there's a healthy dose of contentment and fulfillment she got from nailing that word after the countless hours of study and drilling that no doubt preceded it. Experience has also taught me that the rewards of achieving goals that require genuine effort are far sweeter than those that come easily.

Or maybe spelling simply makes her happy.

All I can say for sure is that when she got that word right, for me, the smile on her adorable little face was eudaemonic.

FAILURE

Elizabeth Gamza

6th grade. Cielo Vista Elementary. Texas.

Failure was not an option. I was beginning sixth grade as the New Kid, but not because I'd just moved—that had happened the year before. A life-changing, culture shock-inducing move from NYC to El Paso, Texas at the start of fourth grade. This year, I was the New Kid because instead of going to fifth grade, I received the "Miss Encyclopedia" award and was sent right to sixth grade. The bar was raised. The gauntlet thrown. And the idea that I could rule the world, being Smart, was set in motion (although, honestly, it had probably been set in motion when I started speaking in full sentences at nine months old). I was smart enough to know that Smart would get me everything. Success. Attention. Friends. Love.

Sixth grade was a whole other level of competition, and my "Miss Encyclopedia" award wasn't impressing anyone. The fact that I skipped a grade not only made me the New Kid, but it also put a target on my back. The sixth-grade resident Smart girl wanted me gone. Or at least to fail miserably. She'd follow me around school, spying on me to gather intel that would bring me down. It was hell. So I pushed Smart out there even more. I was determined to prove myself.

Cue the spelling bee. This would be my opportunity. I could win the whole thing and prove myself once and for all.

The day came and we all shuffled into the cafeteria/auditorium: the all-purpose place that housed any "special" event (nothing about it was special). It always smelled slightly of the last meal, or the upcoming meal, and Pine-Sol. But this was where I would claim my prize. The chairs were lined up auditorium style, facing a makeshift stage with a single podium. The teachers all sat at a folding table, pencils in hand, papers in front of them, directly across from the podium. This was serious business. One by one, we were called up and given a word to spell. One by one, we were sorted to the sides of the room. The kids who spelled their word correctly, and the kids who didn't. I was rapt, silently spelling each word given, being both glad I didn't get that one and wishing my word would be as easy as the one that kid got. The ease of the words seemed to be the luck of the draw. But I was Smart. I was feeling confident.

My turn. I stood at the podium, attention on me. A teacher gave me my word to spell. I asked him to repeat it. He did. Brain fog rolled in, my mouth felt as dry as the El Paso desert, and the big clock on the wall tick-tocked like a giant metronome. I took a breath, shook it off, and attempted to spell a word I had never heard in my life. And I couldn't. My face flushed, my stomach turned somersaults, I wanted to disappear. I made my way off the stage and sat in a cold metal folding chair in the group with the other Failures and pretended I was okay. I wasn't. My nemesis finally had good dirt on me. The brainiac was still sitting on the side with the winners. Gleefully, she caught my eye, stuck out her tongue, and turned back to the front of the room without anyone else noticing. She sat up perfectly straight and pretended to pay attention to the bee. I sank down in my chair, looked at the floor, and traced the linoleum tile edges with my eyes.

When I finally looked up, I saw that most of the kids were sitting with me. There was a big group of us. Each of us coping differently. I noticed two boys trying to contain their laughter about something so they wouldn't get in trouble. They held their hands over their mouths in a valiant effort to keep the sound of their giggles inside. There was a girl pulling incessantly at the threads from the rip in the knee of her jeans, making the rip bigger with every pull. The boy in front of me was kicking the chair of the girl in front of him ever so slightly. She kept turning around to give him a dirty look, but I think she secretly liked the attention. No one was paying attention to me and my loss. They were all in their own worlds.

Then I noticed the girl next to me. She was softly crying but trying desperately to hide her tears and runny nose by wiping them away with her sleeves, one and then the other, until she had trouble finding a dry spot and had to resort to the bottom of her shirt. The resident Smart girl finally misspelled her word and landed four chairs away from me, in the same row, on the loser side. I watched her take her seat, then throw me some side eye and a sneer. I looked at her for a second and then turned back to the girl still weeping beside me. I reached into the pocket of my Levi's, pulled out a wadded tissue, and discreetly handed it to her. She stopped sniffling and took it from me. I heard a quiet thank you as our hands touched. She held my gaze and I held hers. We shared a smile for a moment. A moment that, in the midst of the stinky cafeteria/auditorium, on the loser side of the spelling bee, was an island in the sun. I knew instantly she was my "people." I had found a friend, and so did she.

I don't even remember the word I failed to spell that day.

GLITCH

Dara Padwo-Audick

Teens. Maryland.

I attended Congressional Elementary School and never made it into a spelling bee in those early years or in middle school. Why? Because I am a writer who never knew how to spell.

I had a pen and paper before I learned to use a computer. In high school, I had a typewriter and would carry a pocket dictionary in my purse, so I had quick access to words others seemed to know off the top of their heads. Not only did I not know how to spell, but I also confused words like "affect" and "effect" or "than" and "then" in sentences. These words stymied me every day.

I frequently felt blushingly embarrassed by what seemed to be a malfunction in my brain. The idea of a spelling bee made me want to hide under the nearest desk or run down the hall searching for an unlocked door to the playground where I could swing from the monkey bars and not think about words, any words.

Imagine my surprise and relief when, in my early teens, I discovered that I had a glitch within my physical being. Truth is, I am slightly dyslexic. This awareness hit me like a lightning bolt of freedom. The reason I transpose letters made more sense. The fact that I reread the same sentence repeatedly to find those errors had meaning.

Today, as an adult, I am delighted to spend $12 a month on Grammarly. I teach writing to undergraduate and graduate students and couldn't function without this AI assistance, though sometimes, I don't agree with every suggestion. The best part is that I don't need to apologize for not knowing how to spell. Dyslexia is prevalent, even among writers.

Now, I think of my glitch as part of my creative mojo. And that's an effective way to embrace words, even if I misspell them the first time.

GUARDIAN

Sunee Lyn Foley

5th grade. Beryl Heights Elementary School. California.

It was an in-class spelling bee. I was the first one out. The word was GUARDIAN. The prize was candy.

We had only lived in Redondo Beach for a month or so when school started. In fact, my brother and I had only lived with our mother for less than a year. My mother's parents, Bubbe and Zadde, raised us until then. They were our legal guardians. Though they were extremely loving, the details regarding our custody were kept to the adults. The word "guardian" was only whispered in my grandparents' apartment, probably because they didn't have or know the Yiddish equivalent. I had yet to discover the meaning.

I don't remember who won that day, and I still spell "guardian" wrong on occasion, but I did learn what it meant. I learned I was loved and cared for by my guardian angels, Bubbe and Zadde, when my mother couldn't care for me, and no piece of candy could make that any sweeter.

INDEPENDENT

Angela Harvey

4th grade. St. Casimir's Catholic School. Missouri.

This spelling bee wasn't just any bee, it was the culmination of an academic honors ceremony where I'd swept the certificates in just about every category. The crowd's expectations of me were high, as were my own.

Socially, I was a mess. Physically, I was the opposite of an athlete. Emotionally? A complete disaster. But academically, you couldn't tell me shit. This was MY spelling bee. I knew it. Everybody in the auditorium knew it. But then came the word that humbled me forever: independent. I didn't know it would humble me when I first heard it. I thought it was MY word; a perfect descriptor for my bright future. Then I loudly and boldly spelled it at the mic: I-N-D-E-P-E-N-D-A-N-T.

"Incorrect," the officiant said. My mind swirled. The stage tilted. My mouth dropped. I wanted to argue. But the auditorium was too full for me to make a scene. I went and sat down with my parents, feeling wronged and angry. I still believed I was right.

I believed it for the rest of the spelling bee and the entire drive home. If only we'd had smart phones then.

First thing I did when I got home was open my chocolate brown, hardback Webster's Collegiate Dictionary. And there it was. I-N-D-E-P-E-N-D-E-N-T. It was E. Not A, E.

I hadn't been wronged, I'd been wrong.

Now, way too many years later, I'm operating as an independent artist. After more than a decade working inside studio systems, I've found myself once again on the outside. As the entertainment industry implodes, I find myself scraping dimes against nickels in an effort to make my art. Financially, it's a new kind of hardship.

Creatively, I'm liberated. I'm independent. And I wouldn't have it any other way.

INSUFFERABLE

Nunzio DeFilippis

Age 10. P.S. 22. New York.

To be honest, I don't remember the word I lost on. I don't remember much about the 1981 NYC Spelling Bee except that I definitely should not have been there.

You see, I cheated.

Not at the city-wide bee—that was on a stage in front of a LOT of people, including some reporters. It would have been suicidal to cheat there. But at my elementary school, P.S. 22 (also known as Thomas Jefferson Elementary), the stakes were much lower.

Thing is, I was an okay speller. Not good enough back then to consider it a strength, but I didn't struggle with it either. I *was* terrible at being in a spotlight—something I've worked to overcome over the course of my life, but hadn't made much headway on at the age of 10. So when the school announced a spelling bee, I wasn't interested. But a friend who also liked to tease my little brother (which today would make him a "frenemy") was convinced he was the best speller at the school—better in the fifth grade than even any sixth grader. And I was determined to deny him. Just to do better than him, as a fellow fifth grader. So I signed up for the spelling bee.

Because we had a lot of kids doing it, we got to sit in the audience seats in our auditorium—but spread out far enough to not crowd each other. So I talked to teachers, got a list of likely words and... well, put that list in the armrest of the seat in front of where I'd decided to do the school spelling bee.

Now, the teacher in me looks back and realizes I put more work into cheating than I would have needed to prepare. But, hey, I was too young and stupid (and determined to best my frenemy) to see that.

And it worked. But not in the ways I planned.

I beat him without ever once checking my list. Beat the entire fifth grade, actually. The teacher in me looks back and sees the point at which I could have learned a valuable lesson. Except...nah. It went to my head. I didn't accept this victory. There came a word I didn't remember, but it was written on my list. I can't remember that one either. But I remember reaching for my list. 100% cheating there.

The damn word won me the school spelling bee. Ahead of the sixth graders. And cemented my place among the other students the school would send to the city-wide spelling bee.

I don't remember that word.

I don't remember any of the words I was asked in the city-wide spelling bee—where I was on a stage, where cheating was not possible, and where my anxiety about being in front of people was in overdrive.

I remember nothing about that day except the feeling of having done this to myself. If I had only stayed in my lane and not wanted to put this friend in his place for having dared to mock my little brother. If I had only studied instead of planning this cheating operation as if I were some sort of criminal master-mind. If I had only been satisfied having won the fifth grade but let myself lose on the one word I actually cheated on (though, having won the fifth grade, that might have still led me to the city-wide). If only...

The funniest part? I came in fourth in the city of New York. Fourth! At 10 years old. I became known in my family and their circles as an expert speller.

Wish I could remember what word got me. Or what word won me the bee at my elementary school. Or any of the words I wrote down in preparation to cheat, or any of the words I got correct in a completely above-board way at the city-wide.

Instead, I remember that I cheated, got away with it, then faced unexpected consequences, and then got away with that. And I learned no lesson from it at all. Not back then. In fact, it made me pretty insufferable for a while as a kid.

I-N-S-U-F-F-E-R-A-B-L-E.

JUGGERNAUT

Rhema Boston

Age unknown. Boston Home School Academy. New York.

Spelling bees at my school were a little different. Okay, maybe very different, but I still remember it like it was yesterday...

Palms sweaty, dry mouth, heart racing as I tried to avoid eye contact with all those anticipatory faces, waiting with bated breath for me to fumble my word. I knew they were waiting for my demise because I could distinctly see each and every one of their beady-eyed faces, since my school's "big auditorium" was actually my living room, and my "stage" was standing dead center in the middle of its barf green-colored shaggy carpet.

Those faces? Not school peers, but my four siblings, my mother (who doubled as my teacher, of every subject), and my dad, who often liked to play the role of "Mr. Churchbull" (think *Matilda's* Miss Trunchbull), the religious pastor/principal/dad who would pop in from time to time to see if we sounded like we were having too much fun, to make sure our school work was getting done...

But my dad and his evangelical Bible Belt chokey weren't my adversaries that day. No, on that day, I was too busy focusing on the fact that, after having the word repeated copious times, hearing its definition and in a sentence (which, may I add, didn't make sense), I still had no idea how to spell it, what it meant, or which one of those fuckers picked JUGGERNAUT for me to (mis)spell.

A thousand thoughts ran an ADHD mile a minute through my head as my family waited for my response: *Is the ending like 'all for nought,' or 'tie the knot'? Maybe's it's like 'this is not for me,' and there are no silent letters; after all, silent letters only exist to make bougie smart people feel smarter, or a dumb person feel dumber, not knowing there's a silent letter in that as well...*

Clearly a dumb person made up the word "dumb." They probably came up with "juggernaut," too.

Dumb, dumb, dumb. That's what I was. That's what this whole thing was. And the fact that I wasn't in a real school, just gaslit to stand in an ugly carpeted living room in my house like it was even remotely close to the real thing, was also dumb. But at least I knew how to spell that.

Overthinking my response, this one word was unraveling the threads of my potential future existence. *Maybe I should stop while I'm ahead,* I thought. Or, better yet, not even try. Middle child of five, so it didn't really matter what I did or how much I tried (and boy did I try); I was always going to be invisible. The weird homeschool girl who would do anything to fit in, to be normal, but can't even spell simple dumb words like "juggernaut." How would I ever escape this hell hole and make it in the real world? How would I ever have enough determination, courage, grit, and delusional optimism to move across the country to California and follow my dream if I couldn't even push myself to spell this word? Right or wrong, the part that matters is that I was willing to try, right? No matter how dumb I might look if I fail?

What was I waiting for?

If I don't make the jump now I'll always be stuck in this small town, too afraid to take chances, too afraid to fail, too shy to speak up, too socially anxious to ever get on a plane and see where my dreams could take me. Always overthinking, trapped in this mental prison. Lips trembling, trying to form words, trying to break free of the fate no one could seem to outrun, trying to prove to myself I have the guts to get out there in the real world and not only survive, but actually get a chance to finally live.

On edge, looking down at the long drop to failure, I closed my eyes and dug my toes into the grassy green carpet, grounding myself as I prepared to leap like an astronaut: weightless, defying gravity on an adventure of a lifetime into the unknown, hoping that if I jump, I might never touch the ground again. Honing everything my principal and teacher taught me, and without further thought, I confidently belted out, "J-U-G-G-E-R-N-O-U-G-H-T: JUGGERNAUT."

I misspelled the word, but I made it to California; me, this little homeschooled girl from upstate New York, whose only goal was to not let anything stop her from following her dreams. I'm not sure how I've come this far, but it's safe to say there was some kind of juggernaut-al force that's been pushing and guiding me forward since that day.

KARAOKE

Stefanie Webb

Age 9. Lincoln Elementary School. California

Why would a nine-year-old need to know the word *karaoke*? I was familiar with it as my aunt always pulled out karaoke when she was about six drinks in, but I never partook in it. Now, *Goldschläger*, I could have spelled that—not because I partook, but because I liked the way the bottle looked and memorized every gorgeous detail.

I was nine at Lincoln Elementary School. I wasn't part of the state-wide or even city-wide spelling bee, but in my class, I was about average. Words have never been my "thing." I have one of the worst vocabularies of any writer I know, and I can't spell words like *restaurant* or *silhouette* without a spellchecker. Even with the embarrassment of losing that spelling bee on the word *karaoke*, I never learned how to spell the word. I was scared of it, just like I was scared to *do* karaoke. It took me twenty-seven years and a lot of alcohol (it wasn't Goldschläger; it was Jägermeister) that gave me the courage to perform.

I only did it because my mom had just died; we had a celebration of life, not a funeral, and we wanted to celebrate her and the things she loved, like karaoke. I have a distinct memory of my mom singing "Tubthumping" by Chumbawamba at one of my aunt's very famous gatherings. To this day, my family laughs about the dexterity my mom carried for a woman of her size as she'd fall to the ground every time she'd sing "I get knocked down" and pop up like a jack-in-the-box as she wailed "but I get up again." She loved karaoke and had the confidence of Madonna, Prince, and Weird Al, though she had the talent of none of them.

For Mom, I would do karaoke. I would do one of the things she loved. Even though I was terrified, just like I was as a nine-year-old trying to spell the word karaoke in my class spelling bee, I knew she would have loved it and supported it, just like she did when she was one of the few parents who came to watch the class spelling bee. I can't sing, just like I couldn't spell, but to her, I was a rock star, at nine years old or twenty-seven.

I performed karaoke for the first time at her celebration of life, and I wouldn't stop for three months. On bereavement, my sister and I would spend hours singing karaoke songs, perfecting our set lists as if going on tour, and channeling our grief through the songs we loved and the songs she loved.

Now I never have to spellcheck the word *karaoke*.

KEWPIE

Susan Skvorc

6th grade. Inlet View Elementary. Alaska.

I love words. Reading was my first superpower, and word games were my passion. My grandmother taught me to play scrabble at age eight or nine. In junior high English class, I won all the games we played that involved words. In elementary school, I rarely missed a spelling word. Because I was always reading and had a great memory, spelling never seemed to be a struggle.

My first spelling bee was at North Star Elementary in Anchorage, Alaska, when I was in fourth grade. I came in second place, but I don't remember the words I had to spell. It's been over half a century. Two years later, I was a sixth grader at Inlet View Elementary in the same town. One day a runner was sent to my classroom to fetch our representative to the school wide spelling bee, which was about to begin. My teacher had not prepared for this day and so appointed me on the spot to go down to the multi-purpose room and represent our class in the event.

I won the school spelling bee, was given a nice little trophy with my name and school inscribed upon its brass plate, and would be going to the State Spelling Bee soon after.

At the State Bee, contestants were all seated in folding chairs on the stage at the Sydney Laurence Auditorium in Anchorage. Everyone wore a cardboard placard on a string around their necks, announcing their contestant number in big red numerals. Mine was 13. I tried to not feel unlucky, but still it made me nervous to sit in the front row, labeled with the worst number on stage.

We proceeded through a warmup round, where we could walk up to the microphone, receive a word, ask for definitions and not be eliminated if we misspelled our word. One of my words was "raspberry." I thought I had it made if all the words were that easy. But I was still wearing number 13.

In the third or fourth round, when I walked up to the microphone, I heard the word "cubic." *Oh, how easy.* I repeated the word and the pronouncer said no, "cupid." I repeated that, still another easy word. The pronouncer repeated it again, and gave a definition—a type of doll, as in a "kewpie" doll. I had no idea what that was. I was 11 years old and had never even heard that word. All I could do was give it my best shot; not much more than a wild guess. I spelled it c-u-p-i-e. I was invited to step down and go join the audience.

When I looked up what a kewpie doll was, I was not impressed. It is a creepy looking toy. It was apparently originally designed as a cartoon character in the early 20th century, whose name was derived from the Roman god of love, Cupid. So I was not far off in my spelling. Just last week, I saw a reference to the same on a Facebook post, in which a woman showed a picture of a cute little baby and referred to her as "like a Cupid doll." Apparently this lady would have missed the spelling too.

My spelling bee experience pretty much ended with my defeat, as number 13 in the Anchorage Times Spelling Bee of 1970. But then, over 50 years later, I signed up for the Adult Spelling Bee sponsored by my town's public library, in Wasilla, Alaska. I had heard of it in previous years, but never signed up by the deadline. Then, in 2024, I saw it advertised again and decided to get involved. I was a little worried that I would have to stand up and verbally spell some word that I had never heard of, and would be totally embarrassed to get it wrong.

When I got to the library, I saw several people who were regulars for this annual event. I was the stranger in their midst. Imagine my relief when the instructions were given to the 18 of us in the competition. This would be a written competition. We would hear the word, write it on a card that was labelled with our contestant number (I was 15 this time, not 13), and turn it in within the allotted response time. If we had misspelled it, our number would be announced, and we could continue spelling, but must refrain from submitting our cards for the rest of the bee.

After easily spelling the first few words, I began to realize something. I turned to my neighbor, a former teacher colleague, and asked if these spelling bees always had a theme. She said yes, and I immediately felt a surge of confidence. These words were all botanical terms. I had a degree in Biology! After 15 words, it came down to me and my teacher friend. She misspelled it and I did not. The announcer gave everyone the bonus words that had been reserved in case of ties, to spell just for fun, and I got all of them correct. My reward was a crisp one hundred dollar bill.

Of course, the following year I was asked if I planned to defend my title, to which I responded, "I do indeed!" My librarian friend said she would be bringing her A game. I told her I'd be bringing my only game. This year's theme was Sherlock Holmes, and I wasn't sure I knew 20 words to fit that theme, but I knew enough to win again!

While I spent the (two) hundred dollars, I still have my Inlet View Elementary trophy, and I'm proud to say: I have never ever owned a kewpie doll.

LOQUACIOUS

Alexa Alemanni

Age 11. Barrett Elementary School. Colorado.

I knew the word. And I knew how to spell it. But I got it wrong.

I was 11. Even at that young age, I already had big dreams of being an actor: I was taking voice, and dance, and Shakespeare and Uta Hagen acting classes at the conservatory downtown. I was constantly dancing and singing around my room, practicing my Tony or Oscar speech depending on my mood, and filling my diaries with tortured thoughts of the profound desire for fame and success that I firmly believed was coming my way.

But the reality was, no matter how seriously I took my craft, I wasn't getting the parts I wanted, and my friends, who cared way less, were. My little 11-year-old brain hadn't come around to understanding the subjectiveness of casting. And then I found out about the Spelling Bee.

If you won your school competition, then you went to the regional, and if you won that, you got to go to the Scripps National

Spelling Bee in DC.

Suzanne Butz went to nationals the year before, and now I wanted to, too. Not that I had some deep passion for spelling. Not that Suzanne and I were competitive—we weren't, and Suzanne didn't have a competitive bone in her body. But whenever I had a slumber party at her house she'd just drill these lists of words with her mom, and that's when I had my a-ha moment: *Wait, I just have to memorize words to get on national TV?*

So, basically, the spelling bee is like an audition, but WAY easier, I thought, because as long as I got it right, they had to put me on TV. And then an agent would see my charming face spelling words on TV and give me a TV show just like *Clarissa Explains It All*. Boom, prayers answered! I was gonna become a speller!

Fast forward through months of studying, and there I was at the big moment. It was me, Suzanne, and Chris Perostanaka left on stage, and I got the word *loquacious*. I repeated it, I could see the letters in my head, and then I looked over at Suzanne smiling up at me with her big huge glasses, with nothing but kindness in her eyes, because that's the kind of friend Suzanne was. I don't know if I got it wrong because deep down I knew I had no business taking this from her, or if I did genuinely blank, but I stumbled on that darn A after the Q-U and that was it. My career as a speller was over.

Suzanne made it to the second round of nationals that year, and I was cast as Tweedle-Dee in a production of *Alice in Wonderland*. I was on my way to a great role and a career well served by my loquaciousness, even if I couldn't spell the word.

MATHEMATICS

Scott LaMascus

3rd grade. Hennessey Public School. Oklahoma.

My third-grade year was Mrs. Enz's last year before retirement from Hennessey Public School. That also was the year MATHEMATICS would become my least favorite word, including that pesky E in the middle, silent and deadly if spelling accurately and on command is the key to academic progression.

I couldn't have been blamed if I'd asked why third graders should need to spell the bigger word, when Mrs. Enz could have just asked for MATH. On the other hand, 1970 was the age of the Apollo space failures setting us back from the Kennedy-era victories of American know-how. The Vietnam War wouldn't end. Other revolutions were afoot. Everything was changing, even in rural schools in Oklahoma.

Third was also the year I learned that learning could become ruthless. You could miss the secret, coded meaning of mathematics during math hour and you could miss it during the spelling bee, too. I did both. I don't honestly know if it was the E that tripped me up or my simple inattention. I missed the word during my very first spelling bee, and it put me on the back row of desks and kept me there all year.

My mistakes were so ubiquitous in third grade that I was taken to the optometrist for the first time. Maybe I needed glasses, they thought. To make matters worse, expectations in our school were high, so 1970 was the year the math curriculum leaned heavily into the dreaded word problem. Furthermore, third grade was the year primary education leaned heavily into the division of students into levels of performance. For example, in gym class, instead of playing games as we had the year before—where no one was the winner or where teams won together—in 1970, the gym and Mr. Tiner went all in for the Presidential Fitness challenge. Colored gym shorts sorted us and identified us by our physical fitness levels, which were measured by how many knots on the rope we could climb (among other things). Competition by blue shorts, red shorts, or green shorts would help us beat the Soviets, the adults probably imagined.

For the first six weeks of that year, Mom didn't know about Mathematics Hour or the spelling bees that Mrs. Enz regularly conducted in her room, allowing students to move up in chairs and rows until they were at the head of the room—near her being the best thing she apparently could imagine. When my first-six-weeks report card arrived, Mom learned a lot. Mrs. Enz had built her classroom around competitions in each subject. Hence the spelling bees. Hence the math quiz bowl. Hence the color-coded-reading levels, from stuttering orange-level readers struggling to sound out words to silent-reading olive-green level, whose privileged members were allowed to go to the library with a simple hall pass. In my head, it was all a different competition of sorts. My old, plump, gray teacher was losing badly compared to young Mrs. Kilgarif, my beautiful and kind second grade teacher. Turns out, competitions and New Math did not disguise the essential truth of what was happening in Mrs. Enz's third grade classroom.

Some of us noticed her harsh language and slammed doors for mysterious trips to the office. Small, daily outbursts. I noticed Mrs. Enz went into the cloakroom more than any teacher I'd had so far, retreating for some reason behind the wall of invisibility provided by the long partition which divided our desks from the area for coats, book bags, and galoshes schlumping along the wall of hooks. For some students, her temper and little absences seemed invisible, and they could perform their studies. For others, the fear of her behavior was distracting, at least, and for some of us, it was a paralyzing fog that rarely lifted. My sister, two years older than I, turned out to be one of the former when she'd been in Mrs. Enz's room. She apparently had learned to ignore Mrs. Enz's moods. For her, third grade also turned out to be the year for glasses—nifty cat-eye frames that remain vintage-cute in her photo album Mom made. Blurry vision solved, she soon moved to the top levels and front row. Two years later, when I arrived in Enz World, I was the latter student who could not ignore Mrs. Enz's behaviors. I also was not ready for glasses yet, even if I was a gold-level observer of people.

Mom simply says that every day of third grade, I came home from school downcast, searching for anything to distract myself from thinking about the day. And every night, I cried and resisted going to sleep, dreading to wake up and go back to school, which I had always liked. Every morning that year, Mom reports, I feigned sickness if I could muster the least sniffle in my nose or a tickle in my throat. I don't remember that part, but I remember math-e-matics. That word is burned into my brain by the shame of being sent to the back row and staying there all year.

Now I know better. When numeric values begin to swarm, I grab the calculator app on my phone or use a search engine to find a how-to video. I also know I'm actually pretty good at logic, boolean reasoning, and several other elements of the broad field of math, as it searches for certain types of truths it can see.

But I wouldn't learn that until graduate school. I knew all along, however, that word problems aren't the only problems. If Scott has 13 years of school to learn arithmetic and he dreads it for those 4,745 nights, how many degrees of hatred, shame and loathing will it grow?

Turns out, that was the word problem that really counted.

MNEMONIC

Paul Hostovsky

Age 11, South Mountain Elementary School. New Jersey.

The word that got me eliminated from the second round of the spelling bee when I was in the 5th grade at South Mountain Elementary School in Millburn, New Jersey, was "mnemonic." I wasn't familiar with the word, though I had a fairly impressive vocabulary for an 11-year-old. For example, I'd recently learned the word "epidermis" from my friend Lloyd, who had come up to me on the schoolyard and said, "Your epidermis is showing." Of course I looked down, thinking my fly was open ("epidermis" and "penis" have the same happy ending, after all), and he burst out laughing.

As for "mnemonic," I knew the -monic part because I had a harmonica and could play it passably well, having learned from a camp counselor the previous summer. So I had the second part, the sound part of "mnemonic" down, but not the first part, the memory part, the silent M part, which is so weird and unexpected—and memorable—that you can't forget it. Kind of like the two Ls in Lloyd, though it was hard to say which of those Ls was the silent one.

When I told this story to someone, they suggested there might be a connection between the silent letters of my youth and my vocation as an interpreter for the Deaf. And my avocation as a poet. *Huh? That's quite a stretch,* I thought. First of all, Deaf people are anything but silent—they make a lot of noise—and after a lifetime of making poems, I am still reluctant to claim the title of "poet".

And yet my reticence in that regard is a kind of silence, I guess you could say. And while Deaf people aren't silent, their language of hands and faces, ASL, is full of silent pitfalls for the unsuspecting hearing signer. For example, in ASL, the subject of the sentence is sometimes understood, which means it's not explicitly stated. It's implied. We have that in English, too. Like the implied *you* in "Be quiet." Or the implied *I* in "Thank you." There are all these invisible diacritics in ASL that Deaf people seem to infer and don't need to see spelled out. Like it's there even if you can't see it. Not unlike the M in "mnemonic," which is there even if you can't hear it.

Sometimes, still today, I find myself stumped by Deaf signers, unable to understand them, flummoxed by those invisible silent letters. And while some of my Deaf friends are the most atrocious spellers I know, I'll say this for them: their fingerspelling is gorgeous. Elegant. Eloquent. Those articulate fingers spelling the words out in the air, the silent letters rising up like birds that build their nests in the hands of Deaf people, flitting and darting from sleeve to sleeve, where they sing to this day.

OPTIMISM

Gabriela Revilla Lugo

3rd grade. Saint Joseph's Elementary School. Texas.

I was at Saint Joseph's Elementary. A school that my single mother couldn't afford. The school was in Texas, where my mom had crossed the border with, let's call it, "improper documentation," and where I had overstayed my visa. Everyone spoke English, and I wasn't great at it. But I was optimistic I could learn it, and I did. Even rocked a few spelling bees.

Ironically, optimism was the word that got me out at the third-grade spelling bee. I have often been accused of being an eternal optimist, particularly by my ex-husband. When our marriage didn't work out, I lost my job and my house, but I believed everything would turn around—even if my dinner was now relegated to a five-dollar beer and all-you-can-eat pizza at a nearby bar. It was annoying to everyone around me. And third grade was no different, though it was the first time I learned that optimism, while helpful, doesn't prevent heartbreak.

I had one good friend in the third grade. Her name was Jennifer, and she was the first Jewish person I'd ever met. Where I'm from, Jews were not only non-existent, they were *persona non grata* on account of killing Christ (which, if I may, is not an accurate attribution; the Romans did that).

Jennifer was the nicest. She didn't care that English was my second language; she didn't care that I lived in a duplex with way too many people, or that I didn't have a dad. We did everything together. We even had a crush on the same boy. Let's call him Jim. That tiny Aryan child embodied what America told me was beautiful. He was blonde and blue-eyed, with a killer smile that curled to one side just a little higher than the other, giving the impression of a smirk (and the fact I can recall all of that after four-plus decades should give you an indication of how smitten I was back then). So I did everything I could to become that kind of beautiful American. I straightened my hair, which my mother ironed on the ironing board. I bleached my arm hair and my mustache. (We won't discuss the peroxide incident because I'm still traumatized from the Krusty the Clown jokes). But Jennifer was my cheerleader. It was fun to have the same crush as my best friend. She was certain he wouldn't like her. She had brown, stringy hair and freckles, which, at the time, weren't seen as cute as they are today. We wrote his name a thousand times in our notebooks, and our dolls married him often.

So when he asked to talk after school, I'm pretty sure my heart stopped beating. I could see the disappointment on Jennifer's face when I told her; nevertheless, she took out her lip gloss and dolled me up. When the moment came, Jim looked at me, eyes wide and full of promise, and proceeded to ask me if I might consider...helping him ask my best friend, Jennifer, to be his girlfriend.

I felt so stupid. I didn't look like anyone who movies told us were beautiful, and I certainly wasn't optimistic that would change. I cried. The same year Jim and Jennifer became an item, I misspelled the word that best described me:

O-P-P—

I stopped short. I knew something was wrong. All eyes on me, I ran off the stage, unable to speak. To this day, some family members still have a good laugh about how "cute" that moment was. But it was my worst nightmare, and for a while, it killed my optimism.

Eventually, I became besties with a girl named Bonnie. Bonnie was Black, and I'd never met a Black person before. Where I was from, people were either white or mestizo on our side of the coast. I thought she was so beautiful; she was also shy and thoughtful. She wasn't spending hours straightening her hair like I was. She was just unapologetically herself. She liked to play with me because I recklessly jumped on the monkey bars and kicked Jim's ass at Red Rover.

With Bonnie's help, I had found my optimism again—just in time to be sent back to Nicaragua. Fortunately, Jennifer and I made up before I left. She was just as insecure as I was, and I couldn't begrudge her holding hands with the boy she had had a crush on since preschool. She wasn't the villain of my story; my own insecurity was. So Bonnie, Jennifer, and I had a magical summer, while Jim became a remnant of the school year's past.

Optimism never let me go. Not fully, anyway. Not when I lost writing jobs or scorching romances. Certainly not when, decades later, I was told my infant daughter would likely die due to a rare heart condition (she's nine now). Is that all because of optimism? Who knows.

To be a writer is to continually face rejection, begging for someone to pick you and your work, to *choose* you, to *love* you. But what I've learned is that you have to pick yourself; Bonnie and Jennifer taught me that. (Well, if I'm honest, so did Kelly Taylor on 90210 when she chose neither Brendan nor Dylan). So while rejection may temporarily break my spirit, it will never break my eternal optimism.

PARLIAMENT

Mark Hudis

11th grade. Rye Neck High School. New York.

Fuck the seniors.

My high school had a tradition called "junior/senior day," a storied, one-day fight for school dominance pitting the juniors against the seniors. Events included a basketball game, a parade float competition, and, of course, the quiz bowl. The prize was one year of bragging rights. That's it. No money. No trophies. Just glory.

The quiz bowl was, for me, Mecca. Worth half the available junior/senior day points, it was a chance for nerds to sparkle. In the school's auditorium, four nerd juniors (me and three friends) and four nerd seniors faced off on stage. Our classmates watched nervously as the Quizmaster (our math teacher) asked the first question: "This rough-riding President..." and before he could finish the question, my friend Chris buzzed in: "Teddy Roosevelt." *Correct.* He didn't need to hear another word. "Rough riding" was enough. Chris was smart.

Second question: "Superman fights crime in the city of Metropolis. Where..." and this time, I ambushed: "Gotham City." *Correct.* (The question, I had accurately guessed, would have been "Where does Batman fight crime?") The juniors in the audience cheered, watching the equivalent of a nerd magic trick.

Fuck the seniors.

It went on like this for 10 minutes. My junior pals and I unleashed a cavalcade of correct answers. A torrent of useless nerd information. *Blue anthracite is coal. George Eliot wrote Middlemarch. The capital of Ecuador is Quito.* Our senior counterparts were overwhelmed. It was such a complete beat-down, the Quizmaster suspected we had somehow sneaked a look at the questions in advance (we hadn't.)

About 15 minutes in, the Quizmaster offered up: "Spell *parliament." What a softball,* I thought. *What a gimme.* I buzzed in and rattled off the answer almost as an afterthought, like the question was barely worth my time: "p-a-r-l-i-m-e-n-t." As I prepped for another nerd-on-nerd high-five, I heard a word directed at me I hadn't heard all day: "Incorrect."

Incorrect? Wait, what? Incorrect? *Not* correct? Are you having a stroke, Quizmaster?

He was not having a stroke. I was, in fact, incorrect.

We went on to crush the seniors. And the next year, as seniors, we crushed the juniors. We were the only class in a decade to retire undefeated. You'd think that would be my takeaway—that we came together as a class of jocks and artists and nerds and combined our powers like a posse of acne-covered X-Men to vanquish our rivals. But no. Parliament, as most of you know, is spelled P-A-R-L-I-A-M-E-N-T. There's that sneaky little "a" hiding in the middle. *Parliament.* Par-li-a-ment? I mean, what the hell? A silent 'a'? What kind of sadist spells a word like parliament with a silent 'a'? That's like spelling 'dog' with a silent L.

Yet whenever I see the word, I feel a twinge of gratitude. Because *parliament* taught me a great life lesson: be wary of hubris. Hubris is seductive, born of a feedback loop based in truth. You're good at something, you're rewarded for being good at it, people tell you you're good at it, your confidence increases, you get better at it and you get more adulation and you get better and you think you're invincible and then...

Parliament.

Fuck the seniors?

No.

Fuck Hubris.

Thank you, Parliament.

RECEIVE

April Fulton

Age 10. Hamilton Elementary School. Rhode Island.

RECEIVE is a hard word to take, or R-E-C-I-E-V-E, as I spelled it into the microphone that collected germs from 50 little mouth breathers on the dank and crowded stage in the Hamilton Elementary School multipurpose room in the spring of 1983.

I don't remember exactly, but I'm pretty sure I lost the spelling bee to Robin Huang, who won everything academic at our school. He was also probably the only Chinese kid in North Kingstown, Rhode Island at the time.

I don't know what I was thinking. I know I was sweating under that blue polyester Polly Flinders smock. The "I before E, except after C" rhyme applies to "receive." Maybe I was reaching for something more grand—BELIEVE, ACHIEVE—words on sappy posters that line elementary school hallways and feature stock photos of kittens about to fall to their deaths from trees or bookshelves or whatever.

At least I wasn't as embarrassed as my friend, who was eliminated from the spelling bee for misspelling her own last name. The principal gave her a sentence for context describing martin the bird, not marten the weasel. Tough break, but she went on to become an English teacher. Go figure.

I still struggle with the word "receive," and not just the spelling. It requires an openness and a willingness and a graciousness to take something offered by someone else. You can receive your First Communion, receive advice on how to be a better parent, receive a hug from someone you don't really like. While the object is usually offered in good faith, how we respond as a receiver is often how we are judged, or at least, how we judge ourselves.

What if I don't really believe this is the body of Christ? Why do I need advice from the person whose kid is about to go to reform school? Do I have to let him touch me? Hard questions go racing through my mind as I weigh the benefits of receiving something I don't know that I want. But the moment usually demands a split-second response, so I decide:

It's better to give than feel fake.

RESTAURANT

Ariella Radwin

3rd grade. Jewish Studies Institute. California.

I knew that there was a "u" in the word somewhere, so I thought of the rhyming words "gaunt" and "haunt" and got out.

When I grew up, we rarely ate at restaurants. I learned early on to calculate the cost of spaghetti at home (pennies) versus the cost of having it served to you (don't be misled by the price on the menu, because you have to add tax and tip). On occasions that we splurged and went out to dinner, none of us would order drinks or appetizers, which could easily double the bill.

We weren't poor and our family could have afforded it, in much the same way that we could have flushed some cash down the toilet. But dollars frittered away foolishly would never have the chance to grow with compound interest.

I wonder now if there aren't more generous ways to go through life. Ways that involve spending money (perhaps even wasting it), in order to have a good time.

Last week, our family of six found ourselves near a cute downtown area, where cafe tables dotted pedestrian walkways. Although we had plenty of food at home, we sat down at a restaurant, all of us together. The kids ordered lemonades and French fries, crepes and omelettes. They asked if they could order dessert too.

Pedestrians walked by, wandering into bookstores and holding boba drinks, and a soft warm breeze wafted around us. I looked at my husband, and he looked happy. My children looked happy.

I thought to myself, with some satisfaction: even the little one can spell "restaurant."

SALAMANDER

Grace Ward

1st grade. Franklin Elementary School. Idaho.

I wasn't invited to participate in my school's spelling bee because I'm dyslexic, and my reading scores were too low (like, way too low). I sat on the floor of our gym-a-cafe-torium, watching and following along in my head. The word that would have eliminated me was SALAMANDER. Ironically, I could have told you fifteen facts about the Idaho Giant Salamander—our state amphibian. I'd recently gone to Reptile Camp, which is proof that even if your kid can't read, they can still turn out really weird. My parents were great sports about it.

Reading groups in my first-grade class were organized by color. The Silver Group sat at the table closest to Mrs. Gibbon's desk. They were reading *The Magic Treehouse,* and I was extremely jealous because I thought the cover art was gorgeous. Even at six, I could use words like *gorgeous* but never spell them. The Green Group got picture books, and the Yellow Group got copies of National Geographic Kids to comb through. I was in the Brown Group. We were the ones still stuck learning the difference between lowercase b and lowercase d.

I remember pretending to know how to read. I'd hold the book up to my face, squinting like I saw other kids do. I'd pretend to sound out words. I relished pages with pictures. Honestly, I loved books. Since I couldn't read, I imagined my own stories—which meant they were always exactly the kind of stories I wanted to read.

Between second and third grade, my school closed down, and I was sent to a new elementary school. My parents must have made the executive decision not to tell my new teachers I was one of the dumb kids. I got a second chance. By the middle of third grade, I could read a chapter book all on my own. I'd hide behind the playground to catch up on *The Magic Treehouse* books I'd missed.

Eventually, I did learn how to spell salamander—but my new school didn't have a spelling bee. My one and only shot was first grade. I'd been stuck in the Brown Group, watching from the sidelines.

This story does have a happy ending, though. It ends with that same kid who couldn't spell salamander (or her own name) getting an MFA in Creative Writing and building a career as a professional screenwriter and librettist. It ends with that kid from the Brown Group becoming a published author. It ends with me apologizing to my manager for my terrible, dyslexic-ass spelling, only for him to say, "Grace, we have interns for that."

SOUGHT

Diana Dinerman

4th grade. Thomas Jefferson Elementary School. Virginia.

The first hard word I spelled correctly was *sought*. S-O-U-G-H-T. I was in the fourth grade at Thomas Jefferson Elementary School, where Ms. Cunningham lined us up against a classroom wall and pelted us with words to spell.

The longer I played the game, the higher the stakes became. The longer I stood against that wall, the more people would see me make a mistake. And I could feel a mistake coming.

When she called my name, I flipped the switch at the nape of my neck: I was on.

She called out the word: SOUGHT.

I didn't know what it meant. Hot-cheeked, I said:

S-O-U-G- H-T.

We were both surprised I got it right.

I am a naturally terrible speller. *Desperate, conscious, con-*

science, weird, definitely, and *unnecessary* are just a few of the words I never spell correctly unassisted.

I write and read every day. But I cannot intuitively spell. It's the same part of my brain that balks at long division. There's some formula to spelling that I refuse to comit to. Yes, that word is missing an M. I can't spell *commit* or *commitment,* either.

Some people have an eye for misspellings. I don't have the eye. I have the ear. When I read, I hear the sentence.

S-O-U-G-H-T. As in *sought after.* As in *to look for something,* as in *seeking,* as in *an attempt or desire to obtain or achieve.* Sought: Attempted to find.

It is a word that has pushed me forward my whole life.

I did well in the spelling bee that day, but I wasn't excelling in school. Ms. Cunningham told my mother she was concerned about my reading and writing. My mother set up an appointment with a specialist for an aptitude test. On Saturday morning, we went to a lady's house, and she administered a test. It contained vocabulary words and simple writing exercises.

The results showed that I was reading at the same level as a college student and had no cognitive challenges. I was bored out of my seeking mind. I sought far more than I was getting at school.

Twenty-five years later, I was in a PhD program for American History. The same inability to focus that I had in fourth grade returned. I was passionate about my work, driven, and committed. (I got the two Ms that time.) But there, in my basement apartment in Minneapolis (the first time I typed that word, it was missing an O), I couldn't concentrate on the assigned readings.

I thought I had an undiagnosed attention deficit problem. I got tested to confirm it. I spent half a day at an educational testing center doing word puzzles, memory exercises, and following a white dot on the screen, which flashed at different intervals, to test how long I could focus. The results came in one week later:

I did not have ADD or ADHD.

I was B-O-R-E-D and D-E-P-R-E-S-S-E-D.

Two words I've never had trouble spelling. Boredom and depression can make it difficult to focus, but I didn't have a disorder. I thought as soon as I started my Ph.D., everything in my life would get better. I had a plan and a map. But I was in the wrong lane. The reason I struggled with the readings was simple: History wasn't what I wanted to read. Or write. I emulated academic writing well. I knew what to do and how to sound. But I didn't connect with it. I wasn't proud of it. There was no ME, as in M-E, in it.

It wasn't what I *sought*.

I never wanted to be a Historian. I arrived at an academic career through elimination, by removing all the other options around me. I'm an intuitive editor, and being a professor made an elegant sentence of my life. But the sentence wasn't true. I wanted to write creatively. I wanted my writing to vibrate in the bodies of other people. The point of being in a field of scholarship is to be in conversation with other scholars. But I was in the wrong conversation.

Once I sought conversation with myself, my own thoughts proved to be some of the most fulfilling company I've had in life. That's one reason I'm a writer. A writer is a person in a long conversation with herself. Sometimes we invite other people into the conversation.

That's why you're here.

SPAGHETTI

Justin Clarel

5th grade. Lindenwold Middle School. New Jersey.

I fidgeted, nervous under the stage lights. Unlike the excitement that filled the dark auditorium during a talent show dance to "Bootylicious," tension radiated through the space. I was competing in my first and only spelling bee, and only two of us remained.

My word was SPAGHETTI. I stumbled through my attempt, probably forgetting the pesky "h." Through the buzz of embarrassment, I heard my opponent spell his word correctly. The kind, bright boy beside me won. I steamed with shame. I fumbled such an easy word. How could I misspell something as basic and universal as this beloved pasta? I spiraled and wallowed until a realization bubbled to the surface:

I couldn't even eat spaghetti.

Five years before the competition, a doctor diagnosed my younger brother and I with too many food allergies: wheat, rye, dairy, chocolate, peanuts, soy, egg whites, and more. We sliced school pizza, birthday cake, and soft pretzels from our diets. During school lunch, I sheepishly spooned rice milk butterscotch pudding and nibbled gluten-free cashew butter sandwiches. At home, I savored dried papaya from the health food store and whisked together blueberry pancake batter with rice flour, rice milk, and just the yolks of the eggs. With allergy-friendly options scarce in stores and restaurants, my family crafted inventive, satisfying meals for us.

Spaghetti, however, was not one of them.

My sadness assuaged by food sensitivities, I embraced second place. Though our doctors alleged we no longer had allergies a few years later, dietary restrictions followed me. I committed to veganism as soon as I stepped into adulthood while wheat and gluten remain nemeses. Luckily, my food-word flub at age 10 didn't prevent me from learning how to cook, and accurately spell, delicious new dishes. I learned to curate recipes to nourish family and friends with nutritional access needs. My adventures in gastronomic accommodation set the stage for my current commitment to disability justice and continued masking to protect my communities during the ongoing pandemic, even when most people have moved on.

While a wheat allergy may have lost me a first place trophy, my food intolerances helped shape me into a creative, flexible, and empathetic adult. Even if I still don't eat spaghetti.

THEIR

Alyson Shelton

4th grade. Newport Elementary School. California.

I misspelled *their*.

I spelled it T-H-I-E-R.

Oooof. Rookie mistake. Embarrassing. So deeply embarrassing to 10-year-old me.

It was 1984 and I was in fourth grade. And I easily knew how to spell *their*. I had spelled it successfully on countless spelling tests, but when I was forced to spell it out loud and the adrenaline flooded my system—I can still hear my heartbeat in my ears—I flubbed.

In spite of my error, I still received the bronze medal (not bad) in the spelling event. We were incredibly hyped up on Olympic energy, 'cause like I said, it was 1984. I lived in Southern California and Newport Elementary School created its own Olympic games just for us; complete with math, spelling, running, and field events. We even had a celebrity guest—a speed walker who demonstrated all of the nuances of a sport no elementary school-aged child can take seriously.

And we received medals of what my child brain only saw as shiny and valuable, but what was clearly clay covered in craft paint. And I desperately needed a gold medal sweep to prove my worth as a person—anything else would be failure. I did get the gold in math but the bronze in spelling felt like a mortal blow.

Some grown-up, trying to comfort me while I held back tears, said, "Well honey, you're just not good at spelling out loud. It's not a big deal."

And I just accepted that as the truth.

As I grew up, I did that again and again. Accepted as truth something an adult said to me in passing. Or repeatedly.

In college, my poetry professor tells me, "You're a good writer, but you're not a poet."

And I think, sure, I've loved poetry for years, but she's an authority, so I'll let that go.

My dad tells me, a lot—what feels like constantly—after I go through puberty,

"You're hefty."

"You're big."

"Too big."

I think, OK, I can either stop eating and be "attractive" or be myself and be "unattractive." So unattractive it is.

I wanted success. Or acceptance. Or happiness. Or all of the above, and I believed if I followed the rules meticulously, I just might get the gold medal in life. I know now, there is no gold medal in life, and if there was, it's certainly not "won" by following someone else's rules. I have reclaimed poetry and my body and its strength. I'm doing quite a bit of that. Taking back what I so willingly gave away.

Which is all to say, I might be good at spelling out loud. I've never considered it a life skill, but I have, for four decades, accepted: I'm bad at it. But maybe, I'm not. Maybe it was a bad day and I was 10.

So *their*.

TOMORROW

N. Eleanor Campbell

Adulthood. Oregon.

My favorite description of the English language is that English is not a language, but five dialects in a trench coat. Thus I choose to blame the entire language for that fact that I can't spell for shit.

Just recently, I was going over a paper by a child who had misspelled *capture* "C-A-P-C-H-E-R." Being a professional writing tutor, I knew that capture had a "t" in it. Knowing this, I corrected their attempt to "C-A-P-T-C-H-E-R." Which I think *captchers* the essence of my struggle.

In my defense, I didn't receive formal education in reading and writing English until I was eight. Before that, I knew only the beauty of phonetically spelled Spanish words. Spanish has rules, English has "I before E except after C and when it says A as in neighbor and weigh and when it doesn't for... reasons." Because Spanish is phonetic, Spanish schools don't tend to have spelling bees, and I avoided that particular public humiliation as a child. However, as an adult, when I got my first smart phone, I was graced with an equally embarrassing, though thankfully more private, misspelling situation.

The earliest iterations of autocorrect used simple algorithms to identify misspelled words and correct them. But when those algorithms consistently failed to recognize obscure names, there was pushback that the autocorrect functions were biased against anyone named outside of Anglo-Saxon naming conventions. So the next generation included algorithms that tried to learn any proper nouns that the user typed on a regular basis.

It wasn't long before I had misspelled "tomorrow" so many times that my phone's autocorrect decided that "T-O-M-M-O-R-O-W" was the correct spelling of the word. So instead of fixing "tommorow," my phone began to change even the correctly spelled "tomorrow" to the word I had invented.

When I complained about this to my father, lamenting that English wasn't just phonetic like Spanish, he asked "phonetic for whom?" He pointed out one of the things that makes English so special is the number of regional accents. English, American, Scottish, Australian, to name but a few categories, and even those have uncounted sub-accents within. If English were spelled phonetically, each of these regions would have different spellings and it would impede, rather than promote, communication across countries.

Not only across distance, but also across time.

Take "knight" for instance. There is no modern dialect that would consider this a phonetic spelling. But past dialects did. The fact that our spelling retains these fossils of previous pronunciations is exactly what allows us to still read the works of past writers whose spoken words we would be unable to recognize today.

Thus English's greatest source of frustration is also its greatest strength. The lack of phonetic spelling allows us to write words that can be understood all around the English speaking world, and to read the works of authors from hundreds of years ago.

And to know our own words will yet be legible to the readers of tomorrow.

UNAVAILABLE

Simon Petty

Undergraduate. Robinson College. Cambridge, England.

We didn't have spelling bees in England when I was growing up in the late 70s and early 80s. They may have become a popular cultural import in the decades since, like TikTok and Trick-or-Treating, but back then, we had written spelling tests in class, and that was it—no public contests or tournaments. That kind of performative competitiveness at school was frowned upon, and would have been seen by the establishment to be just "not cricket" (unless we were playing cricket itself, of course, which, like all school sport, was conducted with a quasi-religious gravitas).

I was a bookish kid. Aged nine or so at Hurst Methodist Junior School, my visual memory skills earned me a place on the Nature Quiz team, but despite my voracious appetite for reading, I couldn't spell for toffee. I could happily identify a blurry flashcard of a Long-Tailed Tit, but when it came to spelling, I mangled the simplest of words Mr. Redfern could throw at us. I remember him saying "I before E except after C, Simon, come on!"

"What about *science*, then?" I wanted to respond, but bringing up another discipline for which I showed little natural aptitude might have been counterproductive. I struggled on, and his cajoling must have paid off, because at age 11, I passed the entrance exam for Manchester Grammar School. This was a prestigious all-boys secondary school, known for its academic record of sending more pupils to Oxford and Cambridge than any other in the UK. Mum and Dad made such a fuss of me, they gave me a Coke and it wasn't even Sunday.

In the creative writing section of the exam, I had written a poem about a cat fight, the only couplet of which I can remember being "a bucket of water / did what it oughta," the cheekiness of which must have outweighed the fact that I probably spelt it "a buckit of warter / did what it orter." It's important to remember that my entire academic career was conducted pre-computer, so my misspellings were only corrected by teachers, slowly over time, one by one; successfully in most cases, but one or two words slipped through the net into my late teens. This couldn't happen today with the ubiquitous spell-check feature on every device I own, but I'm ashamed to admit, seven years on from the cat poem, when I popped out of the other end of the exam factory and (as promised) into Robinson College, Cambridge, I still couldn't spell the word "unavailable."

Not only that, I couldn't say it either, and worse still, I didn't know I didn't know. For some reason, I thought it contained a D, "unavaidable," so this is how I pronounced it and wrote it too. This schoolboy error must have been masked in my written work by my loopy and semi-illegible cursive, which often even I had trouble decoding. All the way through to my graduation from university in 1989, the only typed work I handed in was my dissertation, so "unavaidable" went unnoticed, buried in my fountain pen scrawl.

While at Cambridge I met my first serious girlfriend, and our star-crossed love burned bright and tempestuously throughout our undergraduate years. She was also taking an English degree, but at the Polytechnic of North London, so the discrepancy between our higher education experiences was the source of both weekend visit delight and class war resentment. We both loved to be in Cambridge whenever she could make the train trip north, but for every romantic stroll across the Bridge of Sighs, there was an angry no-holds-barred argument. Jealousy, both sexual and circumstantial, undermined every aspect of our relationship. Essentially, we were both too young and emotionally ill-equipped for the intensity of our feelings, so we fought like cats and dogs, with no metaphorical bucket of water to stop us.

Against this background, her delight at the discovery of my inability to say or spell a common English word knew no bounds. I was already suffering from a certain amount of imposter syndrome, so I felt the humiliation particularly keenly.

"Unavai-D-able?! Un-avade-able?!" she cried in her lovely east Manchester accent. I can hear it still.

We broke up soon after graduation, and I began a three-decades-long career of being found emotionally unavailable by each of my subsequent romantic partners. She was in no way to blame for this, but I do wonder if I subconsciously tripped up on this word in my formative years for a more nebulous reason than simple ignorance. Hard to say so many years later; my younger self is currently *unavaidable* for comment.

VILLAINOUS

Sharon Freedman

4th grade, Read Elementary School. Connecticut.

"Your word, Sharon May, is *villainous.*"

My whole body was shaking. I hated spelling bees. "V-I-L-A-N-O-U-S," I said, loud and clear. I wasn't even close. Forget missing the double 'l', it never occurred to me there was an 'i' in *villainous*.

That was the day I started and continued to hate spelling bees. To me, *they* were *villainous*. Fast forward several years later to a fourth grade spelling bee in Baltimore, Maryland where my daughter was out for spelling "address" with only one 'd,' and two years later in the same school on the same stage my son goofed on the word *supper*. Yes, he spelled it with one 'p,' not two. Clearly, missing double letters ran in the family. Then it was in Brookline, Mass several years later when both of my grandsons were out. I was so disgusted by the villainy of spelling bees, I can't remember which words they did not spell correctly.

It did not stop there: When I taught sixth grade, a few of my students asked me when we would have a spelling bee. My response was simple: when everyone is a winner instead of a loser.

As a teacher for fifty years, I was never a fan of spelling bees that reward students simply for rote memorization of obscure words. I'm a fairly optimistic person, and I celebrate education and lifelong learning; however, in a game where there is only one winner and too many losers to count, spelling bees are indeed *villainous*.

WASHINGTON

Laura Carpenter

3rd or 4th grade. Casita Elementary School. California.

I was stunned when they told me I got the word wrong. 1) I knew how to spell the name of our first president. 2) Across the quad, I could see the name on a red, white and blue poster hanging from an open door—and it held all the letters that I had said.

"Capital W," the announcer said, smug, and then repeated the spelling I had given.

I sat down, indignant, in disbelief. Mad at the system in which I could spell the word right and still be wrong. How unfair the world was! I was in third, maybe fourth grade, at my over-crowded '80s elementary school, with feathered bangs and so many freckles that people, thinking they were clever, told me one day my face would be one giant freckle and I would have a tan. At the Casita Elementary School Spelling Bee, we gathered on stiff metal and plastic chairs on concrete, surrounded by classrooms that penned us in and offered no easy escape.

Had the teachers told us we had to say if the word was capitalized? Even if they hadn't, I was out, and I never entered another spelling bee.

Nowadays, I'm on the other side of the words, a judge for the Alaska State Spelling Bee, sitting in a heated theater with my reading glasses and a binder of answers. My heart breaks for the kid from a private Christian school who misspells "fellowship," for the one who says "j" when they mean "g" and might never look at a giraffe the same way again, for the ones who fly in from remote villages and get out on their first word, and for all the students whose mouths work faster than their brains, adding a letter that doesn't belong or skipping a letter they know exists.

The rules are clear—capitalization doesn't count. Neither do hyphens, spaces or accents. Only the letters you say into the microphone determine right or wrong. That rule wouldn't have changed my spelling bee trajectory much 35-plus years ago. The kids who win are the ones that study words inside and out, who know words I've never heard of and can deduce spellings of unknown words based on the language of origin.

But perhaps it would have taken me longer to realize how unfair adults and the world can be. I still rankle when people in authority correct me incorrectly. I remain indignant, wanting to be the good girl accepting my loss but unable to because I don't feel I did wrong in the first place.

Except, did I spell the word from my memory? Or was I looking at that patriotic poster on the door?

XENOPHOBIA

Maureen Lewis

Age 10. Our Lady of Grace Elementary. Indiana.

I was a goner from the start. *If it sounds like a Z, it should be a Z*, I thought. But it wasn't, and I got out in the first round.

Thanks to that early loss, the word XENOPHOBIA has always stuck with me. I love to travel and I am obsessed with the news. Having lived a full 82 years, I've traveled quite a bit and I've lived through a lot of news events. I'm curious about the world and have decided that people fall into two categories: People who are curious and open, and xenophobic people.

I lived through the Cold War, when the United States was afraid of the Soviet Union. I lived through the Korean War, the Vietnam War, Watergate, the Gulf War and many other events caused by xenophobia. I am sorry to say that I am currently living in a time where xenophobia is at an all-time high in the United States, so much so that probably every child can spell the word with no issues. Xenophobia is a terrible word with a terrible meaning.

If only my third grade teacher had given me the word *love*.

I can spell love.

Afterword

We all make mistakes. We're human, deliciously flawed, and messy works in progress. But it's what we do with those mistakes, setbacks, and bumps in the road that define us. Next time you make a mistake, think about using it as a learned experience, and imagine the possibilities...

Contributors

Alexa Alemanni is most well known for playing Allison on the Emmy-winning AMC Drama *Mad Men*. As a writer, she staffed on TNT's hit show *The Librarians*, and has had original features set up at UCP for USA, Level Forward, and Prodigal Films. Currently she has multiple active projects with Sony, Netflix, and Black Label Media. Alexa runs her own writing studio, Bad Pitch Writers Lab, and is an Adjunct at USC. She was recently a contributing writer to *The Sentences That Create Us: Crafting a Writers' Life In Prison*. She is a graduate of Vassar College with a degree in theater and history.

Alyson Shelton is an award winning screenwriter and essayist. Her writing is widely published at outlets including *The New York Times, Ms.,* and *The Rumpus*. She's anthologized in *No Contact: Writers on Estrangement (Catapult), Root Cause: Stories of Health, Harm and Reclaiming Our Humanity, Comics Lit: Vol. 1* and *The Loss of a Lifetime: Grieving Siblings Share Stories of Love, Loss, and Hope* (Contributor and Co-Editor). She's best known for her Instagram Live series inspired by George Ella Lyon's poem, "Where I'm From," where she's hosted more than 200 writers. You can learn more at her website, alysonshelton.com.

Angela Harvey is an award-winning screenwriter whose work spans television, short film, and features. While she's an independent filmmaker at heart, she's written and produced hundreds of episodes of television on shows like *Teen Wolf* (MTV), *Station 19* (ABC), and *American Horror Story* (FX). She has also developed new projects in partnership with Berlanti Productions, Bad Robot, Harpo, and others. In addition to her work in entertainment, Angela volunteers with the global anti-poverty agency CARE and sits on the Advocacy Committee of the Television Academy. She lives in Los Angeles with a chihuahua mix named Jersey who is definitely the boss.

April Fulton is a James Beard Award-winning writer and editor who lives in Los Angeles with her husband, sons, and a hungry orange cat. In a previous life, she covered food policy and health care legislation in Washington, D.C., launching NPR's food blog, *The Salt*, in 2012. In addition to NPR, her writing has also appeared in *The Washington Post, National Geographic*, and *Los Angeles Magazine*. April is currently a freelance writer, speaker, and cooking instructor. Follow her on Instagram (@thefoodscribe) and connect on LinkedIn.

Ariella Radwin is a writer in Palo Alto who still thinks in coupons but is learning, slowly, to enjoy the moment. When not doing mental math, she writes about small revelations, scenes of family life, and the ironies and joys of marriage. She has become a much better speller over the years.

Caitlin M.S. Buxbaum is a writer, teacher, and filmmaker from Alaska with an MFA in Creative Writing from Antioch University Los Angeles. Learn more at caitbuxbaum.com.

Colette Freedman is an internationally produced playwright, dramaturg, novelist, and screenwriter. Her films include *Sister Cities, And Then There Was Eve*, and *7,000 Miles*. She was the dramaturg at Carnegie Hall and Drury Lane Theatre for *Mozart Her Story: The New Musical*, and her musical *Bettie Page: Queen of the Pinups* premiered at London's Lyric Theatre in June 2025. She has several published novels which span several genres. Colette is the Dramatic Writing Teaching Faculty at Antioch University, which has been named one of the best screenwriting programs in the country for the last three years. Website: colettefreedman.com.

Dara Padwo-Audick is an award-winning producer, director, and writer of broadcast and educational nonfiction programs and series. She returned to her creative writing roots in 2016, with encouragement from her Antioch University mentors and peers. She's thrilled to contribute to the *Spell Check* anthology and is thankful to Grammarly. She hopes readers will not only resonate with her misspelling history but also find beauty in their own imperfections.

Diana Dinerman is a writer/performer based in Los Angeles. She's been published in *The Los Angeles Times* and *The Sun*. She's received multiple grants for her scholarship on Race and Performance, including the DC Commission for the Arts and Humanities, the Humanities Council, and the Institute for Advanced Study at the University of Minnesota. Diana has been called "One to watch" by *TribeLA* magazine, featured in *Broadway World, The British Comedy Guide,* and *The List UK*. Her solo show *DETOUR: A Show About Changing your Mind* was invited to the Edinburgh Fringe Festival.

Elizabeth Gamza is an actress, a storyteller, a coach, and a lover of fashion, art, her two sons, and every dog she meets. If her life were a tree, her roots were formed in NYC, her trunk in El Paso, TX, and all the branches, leaves, and blossoms in Los Angeles. Elizabeth is always seeking new ways to see and frame her life and the world.

Emily Hagopian loves writing stories about her Armenian family, imperfect female leads, and long, meandering journal entries. She is an alumna of writing workshops with Gotham Writers Workshop and the Moonshot Initiative, and enjoys organizing writing groups with fellow alumni from Antioch University. When she's not writing, Emily can be found running marathons, icing her rapidly declining knees, or being pulled around the block by her 14-year-old Shiba Inu.

Gabriela Revilla Lugo is an award-winning writer, director, and producer whose work spans film, television, and digital media. She co-created *15 Candles* for Peacock/UCP with Tanya Saracho and Selena Gomez, wrote *The Christmas Balloon* for Mattel, and has staffed on ABC's *A Million Little Things* and UCP's *Brujas*. A former undocumented immigrant, Gabriela's stories blend humor, heart, and cultural identity, exploring love, resilience, and belonging. A member of the WGA, PGA, and DGA, she continues to develop feature and television projects championing underrepresented voices and emotionally driven storytelling.

Grace Ward is a playwright, librettist, and screenwriter from the foothills of Boise, Idaho. Raised on the road with her parents' rock band, she writes stories about girlhood, neurodivergence, and women claiming their power. Her work has been developed by theatres and festivals nationwide. She holds an MFA from Antioch University LA, is an alum of the National Theatre Institute, and remains committed to creating bold, funny roles for women.

Jodie Snyder is an MFA candidate at Antioch University Los Angeles who hails from Arizona. Previously a journalist, she is currently revising a mystery/thriller novel while serving as a flash fiction reader for *Lunch Ticket*. She has been published in *Vortex* and has work forthcoming in *Trouble in Tucson*.

Justin Clarel is a Black trans and queer writer, educator, and forever theatre kid committed to pandemic solidarity and collective liberation. Justin writes vibrant Black trans and queer stories to help us build better worlds. They are most proud of their work with sketch comedy team The Rhubarbs, original works for stage and screen, and vegan culinary talents. Born and raised in South Jersey, Justin holds an AB in Sociology from Princeton University. Justin now lives far away in North Jersey with their favorite scientist, cat, and many plant friends. Keep up with their adventures at theeclarel.com.

Kady Ambrose is an award-winning historical fantasy author whose work has also been published in numerous short-story anthologies and magazines, including Woman's World and Bloganozart. Her alter-ego is Lynne Moses, a screenwriter, playwright, and writing coach who taught story development in Los Angeles at UCLA Extension and elsewhere. Get a free novelette and learn more about Kady and her sweet little Yorkie-mix, Saylie, at kadyambrose.com.

Laura Carpenter is a genderqueer writer, Lambda Literary fellow, and *Tin House* alum who lives with their wife and daughter in Anchorage, Alaska, homeland of the Dena'ina peoples. Publications include *The New York Times, The Guardian, The Writer, Anchorage Daily News,* anthologies, and literary publications. When not writing, they can be found running along Alaska mountain trails, singing off-key to alert bears to their presence.

Mark Hudis has written for magazines and TV. He is now old and, if not for his kids, wouldn't get any of the references.

Maureen Lewis is an octogenarian who loves to read, cruise, knit, and spend time with her beloved pug.

N. Eleanor Campbell is a writer, filmmaker, and educator. A geneticist turned storyteller, her passion is defying expectations, challenging assumptions, and empowering underrepresented voices, particularly female and queer stories. She is best known for co-writing *Hey, Man* (2022), producing *Turing Test* (2023) and *Milestones* (2025) and winning the 2024 Kay Snow award with her short script, *The Pursuit of Failure*. Based in the Pacific Northwest, she lives with her cat who may, or may not, be possessed by a demon.

Nunzio DeFilippis has worked as a writer for over two decades. Along with his writing partner (Christina Weir), he was a writer/producer on HBO's *Arliss* and wrote for the Disney Channel series *Kim Possible*. They have had features optioned at multiple companies and studios, and developed a video game and a TV movie. The two are most known for their comics (*New X-Men, Adventures of Superman, Batman Confidential, Dragon Age, Bad Medicine, The Amy Devlin Mysteries*, and *Frenemy of the State*). They both teach screenwriting and recently teamed up with Jenny Sterner to create the narrative podcast *Cheating History*.

Ozzie Rodriguez is an award-winning actor on film, television, stage, and audiobook narration. Rodriguez has an extensive comedy background from schools such as The Groundlings, UCB Los Angeles, and The Pack Theater. As a long-time sketch writer, he performed in many different improvisation and sketch comedy house teams throughout LA. He also writes horror and comedy films, TV episodes, and stage plays.

Paul Hostovsky makes his living in Boston as a sign language interpreter. His poems and essays appear widely online and in print. He has won a Pushcart Prize, two Best of the Net Awards, the FutureCycle Poetry Book Prize, the Muriel Craft Bailey Award, and has been featured on Poetry Daily, Verse Daily, The Writer's Almanac, and the Best American Poetry blog. His latest books are *Pitching for the Apostates* (2023) and *Perfect Disappearances* (2025). Website: paulhostovsky.com.

Rhema Boston is a writer, director, and playwright from Upstate New York, known for her blend of comedy and introspection. With an MFA in Creative Dramatic Writing, she champions overlooked voices through genre-bending storytelling that empowers characters to embrace authenticity and challenge societal norms.

Scott LaMascus is a writer in Oklahoma City. His poetry chapbook, *The Edited Tongue* from Bottlecap Press in Los Angeles, responds to his father's ALS diagnosis and death in 2024. The poems have been discussed and reprinted in *Rare Revolution* magazine, featured in *The Art of Aging* podcast at the University of Pennsylvania, and adopted by Mercy Healthcare for ALS Awareness Month. His debut collection, *Let Other Hounds*, is forthcoming in May 2026 from Fernwood Press in Newberg, OR. He directs the McBride Center for Public Humanities and is a board member of the Federation of States Humanities Councils.

Sharon Freedman is a retired English and reading teacher. She enjoys reading, scrabble, traveling, water exercise, and most of all, spending time with her husband, children, and grandchildren. She has been lucky to be able to travel the world and learn about other cultures than her own. She was born in Connecticut and has lived in Baltimore, Maryland for fifty years.

Simon Petty is a professional musician from England who has lived in Los Angeles since 1999. He has an MFA in Creative Writing from Antioch University Los Angeles and teaches Poetry and Meditation in a women's correctional facility.

Stefanie Webb is a screenwriter, playwright, and director from Southern California. She loves to tell stories about grief, addiction, and old Hollywood through a comedic, female perspective. Growing up with a single mom, her writing often shows compassion and understanding for underrepresented groups. She currently lives in Los Angeles with her cat, Maya Beaumont, and works as a tour guide in the film industry.

Sunee Lyn Foley is a playwright, writer, and teacher with an MFA from Antioch University Los Angeles. She taught Theatre Arts and directed large-scale mainstage productions for over 10 years. Her plays explore ageism, authenticity, and what it means to be true to oneself, and her reach extends to young audiences. Her work appears in *The White Picket Fence: Stories of Individuality as Rebelliousness Collection.*

Susan Skvorc is a retired teacher of math and science and an avid puzzle solver. She enjoys reading and writing when she can sit still, but that can sometimes be a challenge, so she makes sure to ride her bike one or two thousand miles a year and ski through the long Alaska winters. She and her husband Paul have lived in Alaska so long, they cannot live anywhere else. They have two children and three grandchildren, whom they visit when they need to head south. At home, they are at the beck and call of their Jack Russell terrier, Henry.

Teresa Kale is a versatile writer based out of Los Angeles. She has written on television and feature projects for Disney, Hallmark, and Dreamworks, among others. Despite the somewhat eclectic resume, her "wheelhouse" is female-focused dramedies with heart. Also, she hates the term "wheelhouse."

Tracy Mishkin published her first full-length book of poetry, *The Way The Salt Falls*, with Main Street Rag Publishing Company in 2024. A graduate of the MFA program in Creative Writing at Butler University, Tracy has also published three chapbooks, *I Almost Didn't Make It to McDonald's* (Finishing Line Press, 2014), *The Night I Quit Flossing* (Five Oaks Press, 2016), and *This is Still Life* (Brain Mill Press, 2018). She lives in Indianapolis with her family and fewer than 10 cats and dogs. You can read more of her work at her website, tracymishkin.com.

Ty Halton is an unapologetically Black and Queer writer, actor, and dramturg based in the Pacific Northwest. He writes plays, screenplays, essays, short fiction, and poetry. Previous work has been published in *Beyond Words Literary Magazine*, *Neon Mariposa, Afro Literary Magazine*, and elsewhere. He obtained an MFA in Writing & Contemporary Media from Antioch University in 2022.